The Words To The Music Inside My Head

Lyrics And Poems

By

Steven Petty

Front and back covers by George Kramer

Hhtp:// www.amazon.com/author/georgekramer

Library of Congress number: 2025914186

ISBN: 979-8-9900681-1-7

Printed in the USA

Published in the USA

Contact information raventwohearts@outlook.com

Contents

A Tribute to the AFSP
The Indiana Chapter

The purchase of this book is an automatic donation to the American Foundation for Suicide Prevention. 10% of the gross proceeds both from the soft back book and digital sales will go to the Indiana chapter of The American Foundation for Suicide Prevention. This non-profit is close to my heart and is very much needed at this time in history.

People you may know could be very depressed but hide it out of shame. This program gives them someone to call and talk to anonymously. HELP save lives and gives hope to those affected by suicide.

This is their information:

Suicide & Crisis Lifeline
Call or Text: 988 | Chat: 988lifeline.org
Crisis Text Line: Text Hello to 741-741

24/7 Trans lifeline for peer support:
https://translifeline.org/hotline/

24/7 Trevor Project for LGBTQIA+ youth:
https://www.thetrevorproject.org/get-help/

24/7 Black Emotional and Mental Health Collective
(BEAM): https://beam.community/get-help-now/

American Foundation for Suicide Prevention
https://afsp.org/ and https://afsp.org/talkawaythedark

Introduction

The ability to express our thoughts and feelings is not always easy.

A lot of people have trouble putting their feelings into words.

If you can't understand or identify with the message of a poem or lyric, they just become pretty words, but a beautiful melody will make even the simplest lyrics very memorable.

My goal is to create words separate from music that can stand on their own, to reach that connection between the heart and mind.

My latest book is full of emotions some happy some sad and sometimes frustration.

Please give yourself permission to release your emotions whether happy or sad and remember you always have a 988 number to call for help.

Remember you are all worthy and special and you deserve to be heard. **You are not alone.**

Love to all,

Steven

Dedication

This book is dedicated to
Sue, Steven, Heather, Ashley and Helaina

Peace And Love

Peace of mind is what I treasure

Extending kindness to all I see

Accepting others for who they are

Choosing serenity deep in my heart

Evolving into tranquility

Advocating for those who need help

Never taking anything for granted

Deriving joy from helping others

Layers of positive thinking

Offering harmony to everyone

Visualizing a world united

Embracing peace and love

Every Day

Every day there's a never-ending list
Of things that need to be done
Every day I go deeper in debt
A battle I fear that will never be won

But every day I find something
That puts a smile on my face
Because every day my life grows shorter
And there's no time to just stand in place

I try to live for the present
And not dwell on my mistakes in the past
Put away something for my future
And pray it will be enough to last

I wish I had done some things different
But won't let hindsight or regrets kill my drive
Because like it or not my life is what it is
And I feel blessed to just be alive

My Legacy To You

I've worried over you since you were born
I've suffered through your broken hearts
Cried when you cried
Felt your pain when you were down

As I'm getting older, I worry about
What I will leave you when I'm gone
Something to get you through when times are tough
Something for you to hold onto when you feel alone

It's not always about money
Because there's never enough
It's about peace, happiness and Love.
Let Love be the seed for a contented heart
All you have to do is plant it
And your healing will start

Let Love be your shelter
Let it be your stronghold to help you cope
For without Love your load will be heavy
Without Love there is no hope
No matter what problem you need to resolve
Always remember Love conquers all

One Arm Bandits

I'm going down to the banks of Ohio
And throwing my money in
Having a few drinks and hoping my luck will change
Inside that floating den of sin

These one arm bandits have me hypnotized
By their winning sounds and seductive lights
I just know I'm one pull away
From having a successful night

Am I ahead or in a hole
I seem to have lost track
Now I'm just one pull away
From giving all my winnings back

Bad Habits and Comfort Zones

I keep backing myself
Into the corner of "No Excuse"
Now I wonder how many times
God will save my neck from the noose
(chorus)
No guru or self-help book
Can help me find what I lack
It's those bad habits and comfort zones
That seems to always hold me back

A good nature and honest heart
Never helped me to succeed
But I know death and taxes
Are the only things guaranteed

So tomorrow my goal is to win
Even though the deck is stacked
Cause it's those bad habits and comfort zones
That seems to always hold me back
(chorus)
No guru or self-help book
Can help me find what I lack
It's those bad habits and comfort zones
That seems to always hold me back

Living In The Shadows

She lived under a dome
Of suspicion and doubt
The only place she could roam
The only existence she was allowed

She never had a voice
And was never given a choice
She was so afraid to go rouge
She just did as she was told

Her mind will still race
Between the hurt and the hate
For she still lives in the past
Around a love she thought would last

Surviving her silent battles
By living in the shadows
Very few could see
How she longed to break free

Talk Away The Dark: Text or Call 988
Crisis Line Text Hello to 741-741

Say A Prayer For The Innocent

I received that e-mail right before dawn
And it eliminated my ability to provide
I guess I'm nothing but a pawn
In this economic genocide

Too many boundaries have been ignored
Too many lines have been crossed
Now a catastrophic feeling hangs in the air
As if all hope has been lost

Greed fills your eyes and now you can't see
How far from the grace of God you have strayed
But the end doesn't justify the means
And won't wash the innocent blood away

All this anger and hate
Will never make anything great
So, say a prayer for the innocent
Who got caught in the crossfire
Of a war they didn't create

When We Were Magic

Once upon a time
When you were my queen
And I was your king
When time together meant everything

Sneaking away in the afternoon
Intoxicated by the smell of your perfume
We bent and broke the rules of love
We couldn't seem to get enough

Together in a crowded room
We only saw each other
No one else seemed to matter
You and me back in time
When you were all mine

Lost in our fairytale world
When you were my only girl
Long before the world got too real
When love was all we could feel

Once upon a time
When we were magic

The Words To The Music Inside My Head

I have this strong feeling inside
Then stumble to find the right word or phrase
But the thought that keeps me up at night
Is will they ever be heard?

The ultimate pleasure I'll never forget
Is how I touched someone's heart I've never met
So, I strive to find that inner balance
And press on without regret

(chorus)

When it all weighs too heavy on my mind
And my emotions hang by a thread
I run and hide to write down the words
To the music inside my head

Somewhere between the jeers and cheers
I listen to what my heart says to me
But lost in all my tears and fears
I search for a calming melody

(chorus)

When it all weighs too heavy on my mind
And my emotions hang by a thread
I run and hide to write down the words
To the music inside my head

Our Porcelain Hearts Of Youth

I'm always looking over my shoulder
Waiting for the world to end
But I just keep getting older
Now I'm too strange to blend in

Some of my friends stay stoned
Some find comfort in new friends
But I'm better off alone
I'm too afraid to trust again

Maybe they expected more from us
Than they were willing to give
But they instill a fear of dying
Instead of a desire to live

We're a lost generation
Still searching for the truth
Looking for faith to secure our salvation
And save our porcelain hearts of youth

Talk Away The Dark: Text or Call 988
Crisis Line Text Hello to 741-741

The Middle Of Chaos

Somebody turned on a light
And I opened the door
Now nothing feels quite
Like it did before

Don't know where I'm going
Don't know where I've been
Now I'm scared of the silence
of the voice from within

I'm not sure what line I crossed
But I'm in the middle of chaos
Even though I tried
There was nowhere to hide.
I'm just a different breed
And trouble seems to always find me

My failures, my success
It's really all the same
For this is my life, my game.
I'll deal with the bad news
Learn from the bad reviews
Because the only way to win
Is to never cave in

Grandma

A hard life was etched upon her face
And I'd find her melancholy staring into space
I'd wonder what was on her mind
But I was afraid to ask, it was never the right time

Available to me anytime of the day
She always seem to know what to say
Sometimes she would sugarcoat it to give me hope
And younger memories when my mouth held a bar of soap

With unconditional love and a firm hand
She always provided a safe place to land
With so much love I felt secure
And never realized how poor we were

She's been gone so long, yet still I find
The smallest of things bring her to mind
Those memories warm my heart and bring on the tears
I still miss her and wish she was here

White Collar Crime

Your decisions have finally caught up with you
Now you're face to face with fate
You are covered with so many scars
From your lies and selfish hate

You are guilty of so many crimes
Against nature and the common man
There's little chance of recovering
From the consequences at hand

So you try to fake self-pity
But stay defiant to the end
When you plead pure ignorance
And your actions that you try to defend

But deep in your heart
You know the truth about yourself
You sold your soul to the darkness
To quench your thirst for power and wealth

Living Without You

I was going through life existing to see another day
My dreams of true love had simply faded away
But you woke up a part of me I thought was gone
And you made me believe I could do no wrong

We were going to grow old together now I don't know what to do
This disease has taken you away, my whole world was you
I can't seem to get past the shock that you're really gone
And the prison that confines me is my fear of moving on
(chorus)
Now I long for the times when I held you tight
I wish I could go back and relive those nights
You were my forever love and memories are not enough
Will I ever find a way to make through today
Living without you

They say love is an illusion, it's never as it seems
But I miss you so much you're in every dream
What we had was special, everyone around us knew
You were my everything my dream that came true
(chorus)
Now I long for the times when I held you tight
I wish I could go back and relive those nights

You were my forever love and memories are not enough
Will I ever find a way to make it through today
Living without you

Talk Away The Dark: Text or Call 988
Crisis Line Text Hello to 741-741

Sunshine

Serenity is lying alone in the warm sun
Unconscious to the world around me
Nature and I merging as one
Safely tucked away I begin
Hallucinating, I'm on a tropical island.
Impassioned by this daydream I feel
Nothing can interfere with my tranquility
Except… a sluggish group of clouds.

Leap Of Faith

Greedy people made you about money
Then made promises that never came true
Now only a few believe you exist
They don't understand why I still talk to you

I've never been this far before
And I'm shaking to the core
Lord please don't leave me now
Or let me get lost in the crowd

I feel so out of place
Can they see the fear on my face?
This is not just about me
But I'm all everyone sees

I came out of my shell
And took a leap of faith
Now I take a deep breath and exhale
And wonder if I will succeed or fail?

Empty Promise Queen

There are so many feelings I can't explain
As so many desires began to stir
But it all started to change
The very day I met her

(chorus)
She was a self-centered tease
An empty promise queen
And I never had a clue
Cause the girl I thought I knew
Was concealing someone else

You know it hurts to reveal
That I thought it was real
And I didn't understand
I was just another one-night stand

You know the forbidden tastes better
Than what is allowed
Now I go unnoticed
Sentenced to fade into the crowd

(chorus)
She was a self-centered tease

An empty promise queen
But I never had a clue
Cause the girl I thought I knew
Was concealing someone else

Borrowed Time

I stare at my reflection
But I barely recognize the face
The lines of age, the imperfections
Show dreams ignored, years laid to waste

Everything seems so extreme
As if I'm existing in someone else's dream
I've never been afraid of change
But the world around me feels strange

Maybe the world around me feels wrong
Because the world I grew up in is gone
Now I struggle with my great decline
From fear I'm living on borrowed time

If I could go back in time
Would I choose a different way
Or would I again watch my life slip by
And still feel as I do today

I need to face that there's no escape
Cause I live in a world of endless satire
I refuse to let time decide my fate
And avoid all mirrors like a vampire

Talk Away The Dark: Text or Call 988

Crisis Line Text Hello to 741-741

Haiku

Let's Frame It

Bright red and gold leaves
Against a dusty blue-sky
A picturesque scene

Paradise

A small waterfall
Cascades over a steep cliff
Bringing life below

Star light Star Bright

On a clear fall night
Diamonds on black velvet
Fill an endless sky

Spring Air

Fresh Breeze from spring rain
The smell of cherry blossoms
Springtime has returned

The Grandfather I Barely Knew

He served at least 3 years in the Navy
And when he came home, he wasn't the same
Maybe he lost his heart at sea
But he wanted little to do with family

He brought a son into the world that he denied
I could never figure out what that was about
He couldn't look or act more like him if he tried
They were blood related without a doubt

With a gypsy heart and a flask of whiskey
He was a character from a 1940's Noir movie
There were so many questions I wanted to ask
But he would never give me the chance

At times in his own way
He would try to make up for the time that slipped away
He was a cross between realistic fiction
And nonfiction
He was his own Genre

A World Out Of Balance

We're living in a world out of balance
A world that seems detached from right and wrong
Simple actions that we once took for granted
Mystify many as if common sense is gone

People choosing death verses life
Violence is accepted over peace
It's as if our hearts are held in bondage
And confusion prevents its release

Are we so lost in our bad habits
That we can't see disaster straight ahead?
Or are we so consumed in our addictions
That we allow ourselves to be misled?

One day our complications
Will destroy the good we process
Maybe then we'll see those simple things
That made us happy and brought us success

Another Friday Night

It's another Friday night
And nothing is feeling right
By now you've started drinking
And cried so many tears you can't see
And I hear you're blaming it all on me
(chorus)
But I'm still in the pathetic stage
Pouring out my heart page after page
Despite all the shit you put me through
I still don't know how
To fall out of love with you

I saw your post online
Frontin' to your friends you feel free
So, you think getting your nails done
Means you're finally over me?
And you're still telling lies
Creating new alibis
But your insincerity bleeds through
Cause most of this is on you
(chorus)
Cause I'm still in the pathetic stage
Pouring out my heart page after page
Despite all the shit you put me through

I still don't know how

To fall out of love with you

Talk Away The Dark: Text or Call 988

Crisis Line Text Hello to 741-741

The Different Spice

I want to blend in with this crowd
But the silence is very loud
Everyone is excepting and nice
Yet I can tell I'm the different spice

I search for something clever to say
To make this awkward feeling go away
I'm trying to make a positive change
But so far, I just come off as strange

Now my self-conscious monster
Rears its ugly head
And I start to worry about
Everything I've said

This experience, this challenge
Should never make me question why
I know I'll never win if I never try
No matter what the outcome might be
I still and always will believe in me

My Recruitment To Hell

They made their offer, and it felt so right
Like a shining star on a clear black sky
They promised prestige, fortune and fame
But I knew once I committed
My life would never be the same

"You're just the one we've been looking for"
That was my sign to run for the door
Now this special organization
Has turned into an angry mob
What the hell was I thinking
When I took this job

I'm gonna say what I gotta say
I'm no longer worried about your scorn
Cause I've been pissing someone off
Since the day I was born

I know you don't believe your own lies
You're just the overpaid company whore
And the day you stop pretending
Is the day you're out the door

The Glass Ceiling

Equipped with a master's degree
She came to contribute in a positive way.
The business world wasn't what she thought it would be.
But in a man's world there was little she could say.
Entering through the door of opportunity
She became trapped by her desire to succeed.
But she nearly lost her sanity.
In a corporate boardroom of greed.
Her conscience and her home-grown pride
Made her cover her backroom tracks.
But there came a day she could no longer hide
The difference in the lies and the facts.
An internal conflict began to feed
On whom she was and who she wanted to be.
A crossroads in life between want and need
As she realized her ultimate destiny.

Writers Block

I'm stumbling through the dark in frustration
As I blindly search for Motivation
Maybe the magic has begun to fade
Because nothing feels the same

I can't think and my confusion shows
Where are the words that use to flow?
Is the moral support less than it use to be?
I feel abandoned in the middle of my journey

My future seems clouded with uncertainty
Or is it the fear of failure smothering me?
Either way I'm stuck in limbo
Blocking what use to come naturally

Can I climb out of this hole and succeed?
Or will it collapse and bury me?
I'm stuck in neutral with self-doubt
Waiting for Inspiration to bail me out

The Darkest Hour

What's it like to decide the fate of a nation?
What's it like to hear them scream and cry?
Destroying the present and future generations
What's it like to watch the innocent die?
(chorus)
You were there when it all went down
You were there when it all went sour
When no love for life could be found
You were there in the darkest hour

Do you think about it now that it's in the past?
Do you think about it and wonder if you were right?
Those haunting pictures will forever last
Do you think about it when you're alone at night?
(chorus)
You were there when it all went down
You were there when it all went sour
When no love for life could be found
You were there in the darkest hour

Do you wonder how you will be written into history?
Do you wonder if you betrayed your fellow man?
It may take years to solve this mystery
Do you wonder if it was part of the master plan?

(sub-chorus)

You were there acting smug
Pushed the button, pulled the plug
No more cover-ups, no more lies
No more excuses or alibis

Talk Away The Dark: Text or Call 988
Crisis Line Text Hello to 741-741

A Confusing Time

It's getting harder as I age
To live in a world full of rage
It takes all my strength to survive
A confusing time to be alive

On the horizon brews a storm
Unlike anything ever known
Destructive hate begins to form
Incalculable harm is fully shown

I guess it's always been the same
Finding someone innocent to blame
But the threats and lies from the political stage
Is staining my blue-sky beige

Emotionally and spiritually battered
Trying to get past the toxic lies
Where do you put your faith that's shattered?
Just trying not to be the next sacrifice

Four Seasons In Haiku

Rebirth

Foliage comes to life
As rain continues to fall
The magic of spring

Hibernation

Cornfields lie sleeping
Beneath a huge harvest moon
Silent until spring

Summer Pests

Basket full of food
The picnic party is crashed
Uninvited ants

Winter Day

Snow up to my knees
The wind blowing on my neck
The sun in my eye

Broken Promises Broken Dreams

Though you try to ignore me
I know that you care
Still, I find myself searching
For an answer that isn't there
I guess nothing is as it seems
And all I have left
Are broken promises broken dreams

When I wanted to talk you had nothing to say
When I reached for you, you backed away
Now I fight back the tears behind a silent scream
And all I have left
Are broken promises broken dreams

I never thought life would be easy
I never thought it would be a breeze
But I never thought it could be this bad
Cause all I have left
Are broken promises broken dreams

Talk Away The Dark: Text or Call 988
Crisis Line Text Hello to 741-741

Shipwreck

Seaworthy ships are sabotaged by land pirates

Human buzzards who feed off other's misfortune

Imprudent shipwreck salvagers deceitfully

Place lights at the point to draw ships onto the rocks

Weary sailors too trusting on a foggy night

Run unknowingly into their illegal schemes

Eventually drifting to the water's edge

Cursing betrayal of the hidden moon they soon

Know they have been deceived by New World Moon-cursers

To Dream Or Not To Dream

Life is short, don't let it pass you by
Just go all out and get extreme
And don't let the goals of your life
Become just a life in a dream

Don't let other's excessive expectations
Poison your point of view
Don't allow unsolicited obligations
Leave you accepting half-truths

Now I feel I need to make a choice
Brush off fate or listen to my inner voice
It screams at me "dream big never compromise
For fear of living is death's greatest disguise"

My past is behind me
My future is still unknown
Should I chase my dream or move on?
Cause all I really have is today

Fantasy In High Heels

She drifts into the room dressed to thrill
Leading me to assume she has a certain set of skills
A goodtime bottle of wine would ignite dangerous fires
Now fantasy consumes my mind flaming forbidden desires

She sends an "as if" look without hesitation
So, I flash a half-smile in an appeal
To miss fifty shades of temptation
To this fantasy in high heels
　　(Chorus)
She's an attention-grabbing flirt
In a seductive short skirt
Claiming every eye in the room
Sexual tension in full bloom
And I'm left to take the blame
Another victim in this contagious game

I'm glad to know she doesn't care
Cause her assets are at eye view
And I'm trying hard not to stare
But my eyes just won't move
　　(chorus)
She's an attention-grabbing flirt
In a seductive short skirt

Claiming every eye in the room
Sexual tension in full bloom
And I’m left to take the blame
Another victim in this contagious game

It's 3 AM

My mind is an emotional shipwreck
My heart has sunk to the bottom
It's 3 AM
And I'm staring at an empty bottle of gin

My thoughts are a cluttered collection
I'm unable to make a selection
Of what to save and what to let go

As my confusion grows
I worry the cracks in my armor
Are beginning to show
Covered in frustration I hide in self-isolation

Your love mysteriously appeared like a ghost
But then you left me when I needed you most
I'm still confused why it turned out this way
You were always my anker
That kept me from drifting away

Talk Away The Dark: Text or Call 988
Crisis Line Text Hello to 741-741

A Worthy Cause

He joined the cause
It was a masquerade
A way to vent his feelings.
He wanted to change laws
But little impact was made
Due to political wheeling and dealing.
With his back against the wall
His reasoning began to fade
And his anger led to killing.
Now his future stalls
A death sentence is made
But a lawyer is appealing.

The Big Picture

Some live their whole life and never see it
Others see it early in fortune and fame
Most don't believe so they never commit
And live their entire life out of focus, out of frame

Some are so afraid of dying they just stop living
Allowing negativity to destroy their self-worth
Others tend to be selfish always taking, never giving
And they create their own hell here on earth

You have the doomsayers screaming "the end is near"
In a world that is filled with hate and sorrow
People walking around with hearts full of fear
They've given up on a better tomorrow

What is the big picture? Do you even have a clue?
Or are you drifting through life pretending to know?
Will you ever solve the puzzle inside you
That connects your heart, mind and soul.

My Sanctuary

When I need to be alone with my thoughts
I escape to my sacred place
To deal with my emotions without fear
And have the freedom to exist without grace

I know rejection should always be expected
I can't be afraid to fail, or I'll never grow
I need to focus on my progress
And find strength to concentrate on my goals

I need to be who I am, embrace who I am
And ignore those who feel I overachieve
To learn to be myself without shame
And disregard all who don't believe

I need to find a way to make it happen
Learn from setbacks and start again
To never give up or accept defeat
I just need to find another way to win

Miles Apart

Before we met, I never knew love
There were days, you were all I thought of

But the complications of life
Wouldn't let us stay the same
And I cherish our memories too much
To let you take all of the blame

I was hoping if nothing else
We'd accidently "get it together"
Maybe it's just that time of season
Being sad for no reason
    (chorus)
But there's little you can say
When the magic goes away
Gone is the flame, gone is the spark
We've simply drifted miles apart

I wonder if some day
You'll reminisce I was the one that got away
I just know that we really tried
And a part of me feels like I died
    (chorus)
But there's little you can say

When the magic goes away
Gone is the flame, gone is the spark
We've simply drifted miles apart

Talk Away The Dark: Text or Call 988
Crisis Line Text Hello to 741-741

Stealing Time

Time is an entity all its own
It never slows down, it just continues to flow.
Time is endless, but your time allotted is not
Now my time whispers to me memories I forgot

As my allotted time declines
My plan is to steal more time
You see I've been running from death
Since the year 1975

Now I wonder if the voices in my head
Are from the living or the dead
Maybe it's from a distant time
Or am I a "textbook broken mind"?

So, I'm just stealing time
Simply taking what I feel is mine
No matter which way I choose
I figure I have nothing to lose.

I push my luck against the grain
Believing I have everything to gain

Successful Road To Nowhere

I once saw a wise man
Sell his soul and become a mindless slave
In pursuit of greener pastures
He left his conscious in an unmarked grave

Knowledge is useless without action
It can cause a distressed heart to never mend
But you live your whole life in vain
When all you do is chase the wind

When you fill your heart with vanity
The seeds of despair begin to grow
You lie down hungry for life
And awake to an empty soul

You now find you are guilty
Neglecting the ones who deserved your care
And time slips away and you're all alone
On that successful road to nowhere

Books make great gifts

For more copies, please go to my webpage

raven-two-hearts.square.site

To leave comments on my poetry you can e-mail me at:

raventwohearts@outlook.com

About The Author

Steven Petty writes poetry and lyrics. He loves to tell stories. His dedication to helping others is the main reason he writes. He credits his success to his Creator, his family and friends.

He has been published in small press magazines over 70 times and won second place in a song writing contest in 2003 for "The Darkest Hour."

He self- published his first book in 2024 "When My Heart Speaks"
to moderate success, but great satisfaction.

He has been a lifelong fan of Baseball, and his favorite team is the Cincinnati Reds.
He enjoys nature and photography
and can lose track of time when reading about history.

Steven was raised on the East side of Indianapolis, IN
and has tremendous affection for
The Historical Irvington area.

He feels his greatest accomplishment is
being married to his beautiful wife Sue
for over 49 years.

He is very proud of his two children

and two grandchildren who have

inspired and helped him in his writing career.

www.ingramcontent.com/pod-product-compliance
Lightning Source LLC
LaVergne TN
LVHW011052110826
845149LV00015B/3469

* 9 7 9 8 9 9 0 0 6 8 1 1 7 *